BACK TO BACK
CHAMPIONS CUP 2015/16

Photography Matt Impey & Getty Images | **Words** Clare Ludlow | **Design** Tom Dear & Lara Di Ferdinando

£25

Publisher twocan under licence from Saracens ©2017
ISBN: 978-1-911502-28-9
Every effort has been made to ensure the accuracy of information within this publication but the publishers cannot be held responsible for any errors or omissions. Views expressed are those of the author and do not necessarily reflect those of the publishers or the football club. All rights reserved.

SQUAD LIST | 2015/16

Chris Ashton
Richard Barrington
Brad Barritt
Marcelo Bosch
Schalk Brits
Kelly Brown
Jacques Burger
Neil De Kock
Petrus Du Plessis
Nathan Earle
Mike Ellery
Owen Farrell
Catalin Fercu
Juan Figallo
Will Fraser
Jamie George

Rhys Gill
Alex Goode
Jim Hamilton
Matt Hankin
Alistair Hargreaves
Charlie Hodgson
Maro Itoje
Ernst Joubert
Baden Kerr
George Kruis
Kieran Longbottom
Kieran Low
Nils Mordt
Dave Porecki
Ben Ransom
Michael Rhodes

Jared Saunders
Hayden Smith
Ben Spencer
Scott Spurling
Tim Streather
Duncan Taylor
Nick Tompkins
Billy Vunipola
Mako Vunipola
Samuela Vunisa
Richard Wigglesworth
Jackson Wray
Chris Wyles

HISTORY MAKERS
THE STORY OF BACK TO BACK TITLES

On Saturday 13th May 2017 Saracens etched their name into European rugby history as they claimed their second Champions Cup title. Within the space of three years Saracens had gone from beaten finalists in Cardiff, at the hands of three-time winners Toulon, to back-to-back champions themselves. They did it by going 18 games undefeated, vanquishing a string of European giants, and all with a squad whose average age sat firmly in the mid twenties.

Saracens' double journey began with a demolition of three time former champions Toulouse at Allianz Park in November 2015. It was a sign of what was to come. In the 2015/16 season Saracens would triumph over no less than four former champions on their way to the final in Lyon. An impressive pool win in difficult conditions away at Ulster backed up their Toulouse triumph before the Men in Black, who finished the group stages as pool winners, battled with two all English affairs in the knock out stages.

In the quarter finals the north Londoners faced old rivals Northampton Saints, grinding out the win thanks to second half tries from Chris Ashton and Chris Wyles. The semi finals saw Sarries take on Wasps in a nervy encounter where the would-be finalists were forced to dig deep to claw themselves ahead after Wasps took a dramatic early lead. In the end Saracens' experience paid off and a place in the final was theirs. Three weeks later, and in torrid conditions for the time of year, Saracens would claim their first Champions Cup title; Owen Farrell kicking seven penalties to secure his side's triumph.

After that famous final in Lyon Mark McCall told the media: "we truly believe that if we are humble enough and hungry enough – and I know we are – there are more days ahead of us." In the following season his team proved him absolutely right. The 2016/17 campaign kicked off with a historic win in Toulon as Saracens became the first team to inflict a home Champions Cup defeat on the French giants in the history of the competition. From there Saracens never looked back, marching towards the knock out stages with that clinical tendency that so often drives a Champion side. They were ruthless again in the knockouts. A Glasgow side powered by Scotland internationals kept pace for the first hour in the quarters but were eventually outclassed, while in front of a partisan semi final crowd in Dublin Saracens' wolfpack defence proved unbreakable as the Men in Black snatched the game from Munster's grasp.

That season's final in Edinburgh will go down as one of the best; an enthralling occasion which saw two of the finest sides in the competition go toe to toe for 80 minutes. With the wind whipping around Murrayfield Sarries fans were left on the edge of their seats as Clermont trailed by just a point mid way through the second half. It seemed then as if the French side were poised to turn the game. It was not to be however and an Alex Goode try with six minutes to play would eventually secure the win, sending the Saracens faithful in to raptures.

This book is the story of how two historic titles were won but it is also the story of a club, its journey and the unforgettable memories made along the way.

VS TOULOUSE | Allianz Park | 32 - 7
Round 1 | 14th November 2015

MARK MCCALL'S MEN MADE CLEAR THEIR INTENT TO ADD EUROPEAN GLORY TO DOMESTIC SUCCESS

ANDREW GWILYM | *THE GUARDIAN*

VS ULSTER | Kingspan Stadium | 9 - 27
Round 2 | 20th November 2015

VS OYONNAX | Charles Mathon Stadium | 10 - 45
Round 3 | 13th December 2015

VS OYONNAX | Allianz Park | 55 - 13
Round 4 | 19th December 2015

CHRIS ASH[TON] WAS JUST PERFECTIO[N ON THE] RIGHT WIN[G]

STUART BARNES | *THE TIMES*

TON
ABOUT
 ON THE
G

VS ULSTER | Allianz Park | 33 - 17
Round 5 | 16th January 2016

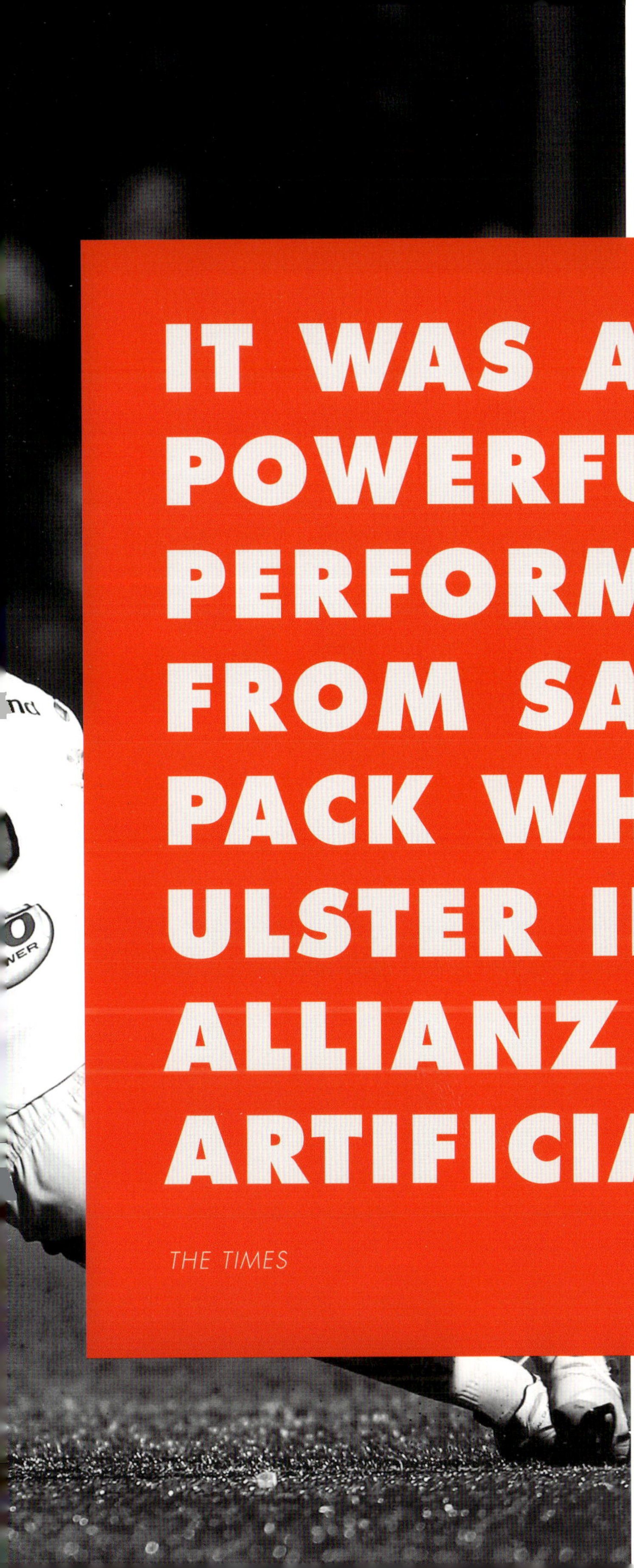

IT WAS A TYPICALLY POWERFUL PERFORMANCE FROM SARACENS' PACK WHO GROUND ULSTER INTO THE ALLIANZ PARK ARTIFICIAL TURF

THE TIMES

VS TOULOUSE | Stade Ernest-Wallon | 17 - 28
Round 6 | 23rd January 2016

VS NORTHAMPTON SAINTS | Allianz Park | 29 - 20
Quarter Final | 9th April 2016

SOME HARD WORDS WERE CLEARLY EXCHANGED IN THE HOME DRESSING ROOM JUDGING BY THE WAY SARACENS BEGAN THE SECOND HALF

MARTIN JOHNSON | *THE TIMES*

VS WASPS | Madjeski Stadium | 24 - 17
Semi Final | 23rd April 2016

A SUNLIT THREADING, PWITH ACTIODRAMA FROTO LAST

EDDIE BUTLER | *THE GUARDIAN*

RILLER IN
ULSATING
N AND
M FIRST

RACING 92 | Grand Stade de Lyon | 21 - 9
Final | 14th May 2016

FOR FIVE LONG YEARS THEY HAVE FLOWN ENGLAND'S FLAG IN EUROPE'S HIGH MOUNTAINS, BUT ONLY NOW ARE THEY ABLE TO PITCH IT AT THE HIGHEST PONT

STEVE JAMES | *THE TELEGRAPH*

IN NUMBERS

33 AVERAGE POINTS SCORED » **28** TOTAL TRIES SCORED » **83%** TACKLE SUCCESS RATE

96 MOST CARRIES **BILLY VUNIPOLA** » **5** TOP TRY SCORER **CHRIS WYLES** » **640** MOST MINUTES PLAYED **CHRIS ASHTON**

86 MOST TACKLES **MAKO VUNIPOLA** » **638** MOST METRES MADE **ALEX GOODE**

IN NUMBERS

ALEX GOODE
MOST METRES MADE
》 **433**

MICHAEL RHODES
MOST TACKLES
》 **92**

MARCELO BOSCH
MOST MINUTES PLAYED
》 **683**

CHRIS ASHTON
TOP TRY SCORER
》 **9**

BILLY VUNIPOLA
MOST CARRIES
》 **80**

TACKLE SUCCESS RATE
》 **79%**

TOTAL TRIES SCORED
》 **29**

AVERAGE POINTS SCORED
》 **30**

IT WAS ONE OF THE GREATEST EVER EUROPEAN FINALS AND FROM IT SARACENS CEMENTED THEIR PLACE AS ONE OF THE GREATEST ENGLISH CLUB SIDES OF THE PROFESSIONAL ERA

GAVIN MAIRS | THE TELEGRAPH

ASM CLERMONT AUVERGNE | BT Murrayfield Stadium | 28 - 17
Final | 13th May 2017

VS MUNSTER RUGBY | 10 - 26 | Aviva Stadium | Semi Final | 22nd April 2017

...ADEMARK
CE BY
NG
FULL OF
PICE

MICK CLEARY | THE TELEGRAPH

IT WAS A T[...] PERFORMAN[...] THE DEFEND[...] CHAMPIONS [...] GRIT AND S[...]

VS GLASGOW WARRIORS | Allianz Park | 38 - 13
Quarter Final | 2nd April 2017

VS TOULON
Allilanz Park | 10 - 3
Round 6 | 21st January 2017

D A WAY, ARK OF S

THEY FOUND IT IS THE A CHAMPION

STEVE JAMES | *THE TIMES*

VS SCARLETS | Parc y Scarlets | 22 - 22
Round 5 | 15th January 2017

VS SALE SHARKS | AJ Bell Stadium | 10 - 24
Round 4 | 18th December 2016

> THE RUTHLESSNESS WITH WHICH THE CHAMPIONS OF EVERYTHING DISPATCHED A HOPELESSLY OUTCLASSED SALE WAS IMPRESSIVE – AND NOT A LITTLE CRUEL
>
> MICHAEL ALYWIN | *THE GUARDIAN*

VS SALE SHARKS | Allianz Park | 50 - 3
Round 3 | 10th December 2016

VS SCARLETS | Allianz Park | 44 - 26
Round 2 | 22nd October 2016

> **TOULON HAD NEVER LOST AT HOME IN THE CHAMPIONS CUP, BUT NEITHER HAD THEY MET A TEAM SO MARKEDLY THEIR SUPERIOR AS SARACENS**
>
> **PAUL REES** | *THE GUARDIAN*

VS TOULON | Stade Félix Mayol | 23 - 31
Round 1 | 15th October 2016

FROM THE CAPTAIN
BRAD BARRITT

The successes of the past two seasons can largely be attributed to the strength of the Saracens culture.

Titles are not won with just the fortunate 23 who take to the field. What we have achieved as a club over the past two seasons is very much down to the relentless hard work and dedication of the greater group, both players and staff, who selflessly make this place unique and special. We have stayed true to our culture throughout and as captain I am unbelievably proud not only of what this group has accomplished, but of the way in which we have gone about doing it.

As we look to the future we know that one of the strengths of this Saracens team is that we are always looking to get better and have players who inspire each other daily. We have a fantastic squad who are hungry and determined, and so we firmly believe that there is much more still to come from this group.

We are always incredibly grateful to our fans who get behind the team, whether it's at home at Allianz Park or on the road, so may I also take this opportunity to thank you for your support over the years.

At Saracens we never speak about goals, or winning titles, we speak about the journey and the memories. This book is a collection of some of the great moments we have shared as a group; I hope you enjoy reliving them.

Best wishes,

Brad

SQUAD LIST | 2016/17

Chris Ashton
Richard Barrington
Brad Barritt
Marcelo Bosch
Schalk Brits
Kelly Brown
Schalk Burger
Joel Conlon
Neil De Kock
Petrus Du Plessis
Nathan Earle
Mike Ellery
Owen Farrell
Mark Flanagan
Juan Figallo
Will Fraser
Jamie George

Alex Goode
Jim Hamilton
Matt Hankin
Maro Itoje
Vincent Koch
George Kruis
Titi Lamositele
Fa'atiga Lemalu
Tom Lindsay
Alex Lozowski
Sean Maitland
Michael Rhodes
Jared Saunders
Will Skelton
Ben Spencer
Scott Spurling
Tim Streather

Duncan Taylor
Nick Tompkins
Billy Vunipola
Mako Vunipola
Samuela Vunisa
Richard Wigglesworth
Jackson Wray
Chris Wyles